The Letter to the Romans

Good news for everyone

John Houghton

Contents

Introduction

Paul's letter to the Romans is the grand opera of Christian belief and behaviour, a lyrical journey through the landscape of faith exploring with uncompromising passion the depths of human depravity and the heights of God's love. Here Jew and Gentile, those two great contenders on the stage of human history, meet their match in the outrageous and unarguable grace of God found in Christ. It is a thrilling theme that echoes down the ages in those resounding chords with which Paul celebrates God's majesty, mystery and magnificence: 'Oh, the depths of the riches of the wisdom and knowledge of God! How unsearchable his judgments, and his paths beyond tracing out! ... For from him and through him and to him are all things. To him be the glory for ever! Amen.'

In this letter God is God and faith is robust. The music refuses to play to the pocket organiser god of modernity programmed and diaried to our convenience, nor to the pop psychology that would see the Christian faith as just one more means of ego enhancement. The living God has inspired a vigorous score that takes love and justice seriously, that proclaims an equality so embracing that no human being can stand outside the frame as a judge, critic or observer. We will each one of us be justified or condemned; we cannot be excused our part.

It is this very equality that opens the curtain for anyone and everyone, irrespective of their historic culture, creed or conduct, to learn the new song of faith and to enter the innumerable company of the redeemed – a colourful carnival procession of those once dead in Adam, now resurrected in Christ and graced with the Spirit of adoption. Not that it is all laughter and celebration; as with any carnival there is pain and death, too. The new creation struggles to birth from the troubled womb of a cosmos yearning for redemption. The dance is performed by novices on a stage cluttered with the debris of the old world. Moving in harmony with the rest of the troupe has to be learned; some of us know only the jerky steps of our former life; some of us are recovering from injuries; a few want the stage all to themselves. By the mercy of God we will all grow to love one another so that with one heart and mouth we may glorify the God and Father of our Lord Jesus Christ.

I have chosen the operatic motif in an attempt to do justice to the vivid drama and lyricism that is often overlooked in the more academic and forensic approaches to this book. Real theology springs from history; revelation is received through the realities and vicissitudes of life, as witness how God spoke through the saga of the Old Testament.

The apostle Paul dictated this libretto around AD 57 while staying in Corinth with Gaius. It was written down by Tertius and taken to Rome by Phoebe, both well-loved members of Paul's apostolic team. Rome, the City of the Seven Hills, was then the largest city on earth, having well over a million inhabitants, as well as being the seat of government for the Empire. Like all great cities it was cosmopolitan and divided between the rich and the poor, the latter consisting mostly of a large slave class. The church in Rome was a typical mixture of Jews and Gentiles drawn from across the social spectrum and meeting in numerous locations. There is no evidence for apostolic foundation; Paul had not yet visited the city and whatever his future role might have been, Peter was still living in Jerusalem when the church began. It most likely owes its origins in part to those Jews who returned to Rome after the Day of Pentecost and in part to the converted traders and travellers who met up with one another in the inns and markets. It reminds us that large urban churches can be birthed without the need to pander to the cult of personality for their success.

Few would have anticipated that religion would be the big issue for the twenty-first-century world, but so it is turning out to be. Whether it is the Balkans, or Northern Ireland, or the Arab–Israeli conflict, or the dispute between India and Pakistan or the secret war between the Muslim terrorist networks and the United States – whatever the purely political considerations – religion plays a major role in all of these theatres. Perhaps the ultimate winner will be that set of beliefs which satisfies both our inner needs and our desire to live in harmony with one another. Possessing neither political power, nor media profile, nor showbiz personalities, the Early Church conquered even the might of Rome. It did so with the straightforward proclamation of the good news of Jesus Christ, articulated through a multitude of unknown voices whose lives bore witness to the testimony of their words. The apostolic mandate, the missionary call, remains the same, as does our confidence in the power of the message to change the lives of men and women around us – 'I am not ashamed of the gospel, because it is the power of God for the salvation of everyone who believes.'

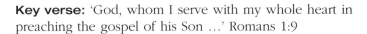

WEEK 1

Good News or What?

Opening Icebreaker

Apart from hearing the gospel, describe briefly the best piece of news that you have ever heard, and why it was.

Bible Readings

- Romans 1:1–17
- John 3:16–21
- 1 Corinthians 15:1–11
- Colossians 1:15–23

Key verse: 'God, whom I serve with my whole heart in preaching the gospel of his Son ...' Romans 1:9

Focus: I am not ashamed of the gospel.

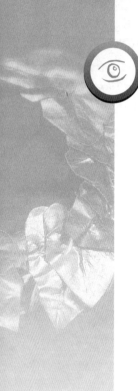

Opening Our Eyes

Paul opens his great work with a fanfare that captures the heart of the gospel message for which he has been set apart and sent to proclaim. This is God's good news, and it's all about Jesus. The Jewish prophets long anticipated the coming of their Messiah, and in a few brief notes we are presented with the credentials of the most amazing Man that ever lived. He is the Son of God, a phrase that implies no less than coequal divinity – the filial expression of the one true and living God, who laid aside His glory to live among us and to die for our iniquities. He has also a human nature that can be traced back to the Messianic promise given long ago to the Israelite king David; furthermore the Holy Spirit has raised Him from the dead – an act of such awesome power that it makes His divinity indisputable. He is Jesus Christ our Lord, appointed by God the Father to be the ultimate political and spiritual ruler over all creation. Recalling a familiar theme – this divine proclamation is issued from the throne of God for the attention of all people (see Colossians 1:23) – Paul reminds his audience of the apostolic mandate. It is to call people from the whole world to submit to the terms of the new government. We see earnest messengers, town criers, broadcasters, writers, minstrels, dramatists, a host of communicators bending their skills and energies to proclaim the good news and the obedience that springs from faith. It is the central motif, the cascading anthem, to which Paul will return again and again: 'The righteous will live by faith.'

Now Paul wants his audience to feel involved in this opera and he shifts from his rousing proclamation to a more pastoral and personal theme: 'God loves you people in Rome; sweet grace and peace to you whom God has made his own. I pray often for you and I dearly want to pay you a visit.'

All roads lead to Rome and for that reason the vibrant faith of this young church had sounded across the ancient world. It seems that Paul's friends in Rome had long encouraged him to visit the church but that circumstances had prevented him from doing so. Some inevitably had begun to question whether he would ever bother. Perhaps Jerusalem or Antioch were more important to him. But Paul really does want to come; he would like to bless them with a spiritual gift and to receive a blessing from them in return. As to whether they were worthy of an apostolic visit, well, Paul feels indebted to all kinds of people, educated Greeks and uneducated barbarians alike. He is no snob; he knows he will find and be at home among both when he does at length get to Rome.

We return to the opening theme: this all-consuming gospel of Jesus Christ. Throughout his travels Paul has seen its effects first hand. Those great missionary journeys have amply demonstrated to him and to his fellow workers that this message possesses an intrinsic power to transform both the Jew and the Gentile. It is the power of God, no less, and it enables people through simple faith to be declared righteous in His holy presence, to find full acceptance and to be at peace with Him, and with one another. Little wonder then that Paul feels privileged to proclaim it with such confidence.

Discussion Starters

1. What do you think the word apostle means? If we have apostles today, as many believe we do, how do you think we would recognise them?

   _____

   _____

   _____

   _____

2. The gospel is good news, literally *evangellon*. Why do you think people consider it bad news nowadays?

   _____

   _____

   _____

   _____

3. Paul tells us that Jesus 'was declared with power to be the Son of God'. What do you think this means?

   _____

   _____

   _____

   _____

4. Consider what it would be like to be a first-century Jew hearing Paul preach in the synagogue.

   _____

   _____

   _____

   _____

5. Paul is at pains to apologise for not yet visiting the Christians at Rome. What does this tell us about his attitude towards God's people?

   _____

   _____

   _____

   _____

6. Paul's desire is to impart some spiritual gift, *charisma pneumatikon*. What do you think he meant?

_____

_____

_____

_____

7. Act out an imaginary conversation with a total pagan whom you wish to introduce to Jesus.

_____

_____

_____

_____

8. Most Christians are at times ashamed to admit the fact. Why do you think this is?

_____

_____

_____

_____

9. Some say that Paul's gospel is too complicated and we need to get back to the simple story of Jesus. What do you think?

_____

_____

_____

_____

10. How would you explain the word 'righteous', as Paul uses it, in today's world?

_____

_____

_____

_____

Personal Application

Paul is a real enthusiast, a man sold out on this glorious message of salvation that fulfils all his Jewish aspirations and transcends both the pagan religions and the secularism of the Greeks. These hundreds of years later, more people than ever are embracing the message with equal fervour. If you have lost your confidence to believe why not pray right now that God will renew your faith?

Paul had not yet reached Rome but that did not stop those young believers from expressing their faith. You don't need a famous preacher; you have a famous Saviour, and He is with you all the time.

Seeing Jesus in the Scriptures

Who is Jesus? A good man, certainly. A great religious teacher, a miracle-worker. A heroic example of self-sacrifice. All of this, for sure, but that at best puts Him top of the league of spiritual leaders, with faith in Him as just one of many options. The Scriptures, however, reveal Him to be much more – He is God's eternal Son.

Yet He is no hologram or ghost. Jesus had a real humanity derived from Mary, His mother. He had the same physical and emotional needs as ourselves; He had to learn as we do, for His brain and body were of the same kind as ours. The miracle of the incarnation is not that Jesus was a heavenly magician in human guise but that He gave up his glory, laid aside His eternal powers and fulfilled a ministry that was done solely by the anointing of the Holy Spirit.

WEEK 2

As Guilty as Hell

Opening Icebreaker

Describe a naughty act that you did as a child that made you feel really guilty.

Bible Readings

- Romans 1:18–3:20
- Psalm 19:1–6
- 2 Thessalonians 1:5–10
- James 2:8–13
- Revelation 20:11–15

Key verse: 'There is no-one righteous, not even one.' Romans 3:10

Focus: The law cannot save you – Romans 3:19–20.

Opening Our Eyes

With a sudden operatic twist the mood changes and the stage darkens. From the glories of Christ we are plunged into the seething mass of wayward humanity, and deep thunder rolls. God is angry. The first two commandments have been breached.

No one really needs God's existence to be proved to them; it is self-evident. The whole creation proclaims His timeless power and divine existence. As the songwriter says, 'The heavens declare the glory of God; the skies proclaim the work of his hands.' Anyone in their right mind will thank God for the wonders of creation.

But wilfully, we suppress the truth, and now across the stage staggers a grotesque parade of idols. Like fools we worship parodies of God's attributes and gods made in our own image, supposing them better than God Himself.

The Creator is no wimp; He feels no need to apologise or to beg for our allegiance. He lets us learn the hard way and as the thunder fades we are left with a terrible lonely silence. The scenes are shocking: lesbian sex, homosexual copulation, an orgy of sexual lust, grasping materialists amassing wealth they can never spend, malicious gossips seeding hate, callous murder, strutting vain egotists boasting their fame, children abusing their parents, bitter enemies, snide God-haters, inventors of vile weapons, violent brawlers and warmongers. The world is full of hypocrites, for they do know right from wrong and they are swift to find fault with others, yet they and their cronies behave no differently.

Our eye is drawn to the archetypal critic, perhaps a self-righteous Pharisee, as Paul had been. Yet the faultfinder may be any one of us who points the finger at others and ignores the three fingers pointing back. We may be no worse than our neighbours but we are certainly no better.

Now the faultfinder is faulted. The throne of God appears, echoing the vision in Daniel 7:9. Our self-righteous man is ruined; God will be utterly fair. We will, each one of us, Jews, Greeks, whoever, be judged by our motives and our actions.

It will be no use pleading our race, our culture or our religion. Everyone has a God-given conscience. We know right from wrong. We make choices.

Paul, in a powerful song of recrimination, takes the self-righteous to task. You claim to be the best, to know the mind of God and understand the rules. You walk the finest path and teach the lesser breeds. In truth you are a liar and a hypocrite. Do not think the removal of a piece of flesh will immunise you from judgment; it is the condition of the heart God looks on. True 'Jewishness' is inner and spiritual.

Passions are roused. 'What's the point of being a Jew?' cries the accused. 'If Jews have failed then surely God has failed.' 'How can He judge us for His mistakes?' another calls. 'Surely if my hypocrisy reveals how true God is, then I have done Him a favour. How can He then condemn me?' whispers a more subtle voice.

'Thrice no!' declaims Paul. There is no excusing ourselves. The uncompromising chords pummel us into reality; we must face the awful sober truth about ourselves. There is no one righteous, not even one. We are ruined, every one of us and we have nothing further to say. The best the law can do, for those privileged to have it, is to raise our consciousness of just how bad we are.

Discussion Starters

1. The Bible teaches us that God is the Creator of all things. Do you think the theory of evolution has disproved His existence?

_____

_____

_____

2. Idols are usually thought of as made of wood or stone. What do you consider are the idols of contemporary society?

_____

_____

_____

3. The passage teaches us that homosexuality is the consequence of a God-forsaken society. How would you share your faith with a member of the gay community?

_____

_____

_____

4. In Matthew 7:3 Jesus uses an illustration from His woodworking days. How do you think it speaks to us about our hypocrisy, judgmental attitudes and blindness to our own failings?

_____

_____

_____

5. Many scoff at the idea of a day of judgment yet we all want justice. Why do you think this is?

_____

_____

_____

6. Salvation is not by works, so why does Paul tell us that we will all be judged by our deeds?

_____

_____

_____

_____

7. Circumcision signalled membership of the faith community. Why is it no longer required for believers to be circumcised?

_____

_____

_____

_____

8. The Jews gave us monotheism and the law of God. How would you talk about Jesus to a Jew?

_____

_____

_____

_____

9. People used to speak of total depravity whereas today they speak of personal deprivation. Just how good or bad do you think we are?

_____

_____

_____

_____

10. If the law cannot save us, why do you think God gave us the law?

_____

_____

_____

_____

Personal Application

This is one of the most uncomfortable parts of the whole Bible because it forces us to take an honest look at our own hearts. People shy away because they don't want the discomfort of feeling guilty. The best most of us manage is to acknowledge that we have a dark side. To avoid the truth we find it easier to criticise others while finding reasons to excuse ourselves. We may even imagine that our social status or education makes us better than our neighbours. It's hypocritical at best.

The first step to real forgiveness and personal transformation is to acknowledge the deceit and wickedness of our own hearts. Jesus told the tale of a man who was too ashamed to raise his face to heaven but won God's blessing by crying, 'God be merciful to a sinner like me.' Have you prayed such a prayer?

Seeing Jesus in the Scriptures

One man has lived differently from the rest of us. Jesus was tempted with all the same temptations that we face but not once did He succumb. Even the most acute critics of His day could find no fault in Him, except that which they concocted. Yet Jesus was no plaster-cast saint. He lived in a real family with a business to run and a trade to perform. He mixed with the rank and file of ordinary humanity, with all its problems, and yet remained pure and true. People loved to have Jesus in their company because He showed them the warmth and attractiveness of real holiness.

WEEK 3

Faith's Big Daddy

Opening Icebreaker

Describe either some aspect that you admired or that you wished for in your earthly father.

Bible Readings

- Romans 3:21–5:21
- Genesis 15:1–7
- Galatians 3:22–29
- Titus 3:3–7

Key verse: 'Therefore, since we have been justified through faith, we have peace with God through our Lord Jesus Christ.' Romans 5:1

Focus: We are all Abraham's children through faith in Christ.

Opening Our Eyes

Paul's sober analysis of human nature gives rise to a plaintive lament: There is no hope for us.

Scarcely the cry before the reply! There is another way. It steals nothing from the integrity of God's character yet it circumvents the impossible demands of the law. Indeed, for those with eyes to see, it was always there, a subtle subtext to the Law and Prophets destined at last to become the dominant theme.

The crucifixion of Christ captures our gaze. We are reminded of the Passover lamb and all those sacrificial offerings that could never in themselves take away sins. Yet now, by sacrificing His own Son, God has exhausted all possible anger, and all demands that justice should be done and be seen to be done. He has satisfied the demands of every lawyer and even the accuser himself is silenced, so that when God declares vindicated, free of all charges brought against them, all those who put their faith in Christ, we nod sagely. It is fair. God has remained just but He has also found a way to redeem us from our overwhelming guilt. The law is satisfied and we are free – justified by faith alone. Pride of race is abolished, history is humbled. Whether Jew or Gentile, we are saved by grace and by grace alone.

The scene shifts to one of period costume and we see a wealthy but childless Bedouin gazing up at the stars. His name is Abraham; he is the father of the Jewish race, a man of gigantic faith who believed God and was declared righteous. Abraham is the genetic source of the line of faith and promise.

Is it then only his legal descendants, the circumcised Jews, that benefit from his faith? No, because Abraham was justified by faith before he was circumcised. So, the descendants of promise are all those who have faith in Jesus – both of the natural direct descendants and those who claim no bloodline but who nevertheless believe.

What faith he had! Well past childbearing age, he and his wife Sarah believe the promise, and the longer they wait the stronger their confidence grows. Faith speeding through the paths of time sees not only a child but the coming day of Christ, the true Seed who will bless the whole world.

The choir may take the stage; rejoicing in the certain expectation of entering God's glorious presence, we are at peace with Him and our hearts are filled with the Holy Spirit of God's love. Even trials are transformed into a training ground to make us strong. Eternally grateful, we recall our former moral weakness; we were not worth another man's life, yet so great is God's love that even while we were His sworn enemies Christ still died in our place. Little wonder we sing and shout with such profound gratitude.

We are talking spiritual genetics. Two men take the stage; the first is named Adam, and he is the archetype of the first creation. His disobedience marked the entry point for sin and condemnation and death – further intensified by the law – so that everyone in his line is doomed.

The second man is Jesus. Through His obedience the gracious gift of justification has entered the world, bringing eternal life to those who believe. The case is made. Where will we take our place? In death-dealing Adam or in life-giving Jesus? Under the futility of the law or in the faith of father Abraham? The consequences of that decision are eternal.

Discussion Starters

1. It is impossible to make sense of the New Testament without reading the Old. Why do you think so many Christians struggle with Part One of their Bibles?

   _____

   _____

   _____

2. Few people today like the idea of God judging us for our personal morality. Why is it that God can't just be a loving Father who lets us off?

   _____

   _____

   _____

   _____

3. Christians are sometimes viewed as self-righteous prigs and hypocrites. Since Paul says that we can't be saved by 'decency', how do you think we can set the record straight?

   _____

   _____

   _____

4. The idea of God crediting us with righteousness just because we believe seems an easy cop-out. How would you answer this charge?

   _____

   _____

   _____

   _____

5. Abraham is described as the father of many nations. What do you think this means?

   _____

   _____

   _____

6. People often lose faith if they don't get quick results. Why was Abraham able to grow in faith the longer he waited?

_____

_____

_____

_____

7. True faith is characterised by perseverance. How do you think we learn to develop staying power?

_____

_____

_____

_____

8. People don't last long without hope. How would you explain Christian hope to a not-yet-believer?

_____

_____

_____

_____

9. We are all stirred by heroism. How much of a hero do you think Jesus was?

_____

_____

_____

_____

10. Paul said that sin entered the world through Adam and salvation came through Jesus. Is it possible to believe that Jesus was a historical person but that Adam wasn't?

_____

_____

_____

_____

Personal Application

God really wants to bless us, that is, to make us truly happy and at peace with Him and ourselves. The promise given in Romans 4:7–8 is that our sins will never be counted against us. The one condition is simple faith in the death of Jesus on our behalf. If you have put your faith in Christ you may be certain that you are fully and unconditionally accepted by God for all eternity. This means that God will always listen to you when you pray. It also means that you may be sure of going to heaven when you die. The inner witness to this is the love of God poured into our hearts by the Holy Spirit. If you are unsure about this then ask Him to grant you this assurance.

Seeing Jesus in the Scriptures

Jesus is the Lamb who was slain for our sins. All the old covenant's legal and ritual requirements find their fulfilment in Him. But He also supersedes them. The writer to the Hebrews demonstrates that Jesus is a better apostle than Moses, a better priest than Aaron, and that He offered a better sacrifice than the blood of animals, in a better tabernacle. In fact, He has made a new and better covenant that grants us full acceptance with God and begins a process of personal transformation so radical that it must be described as a new creation. So Jesus is the Second Adam who dispenses eternal life to all who put their faith in Him. Our new status is then no longer 'in Adam' but 'in Christ'.

WEEK 4

Wanted Dead and Alive

Opening Icebreaker

Describe a close brush with death that you or a close loved one have had and how you felt about it afterwards.

Bible Readings

- Romans 6:1–8:39
- 2 Corinthians 5:14–17
- Galatians 5:13–18
- Ephesians 4:17–24

Key verse: '… through Christ Jesus the law of the Spirit of life set me free from the law of sin and death.' Romans 8:2

Focus: Love conquers all. Romans 8:37–39

Opening Our Eyes

Taking centre stage Paul raises his arms to celebrate eternal life through Jesus Christ. However, the argument is not over. Three hawkish inquisitors challenge the idea of salvation through faith alone.

The first: 'If grace delights to outdo sin, surely we should keep sinning to give grace greater scope. Your message encourages evil behaviour!'
Answer: Remember your baptism into Christ. We died to sin's power as surely as Jesus did; we rose to a new life freed from sin's domination as certainly as Christ did. Faith is not a mere decision to change sides; it effects a vital spiritual union with Christ that simultaneously frees us from our union to Adam and the power of sin and death. Now freed, our bodies are no longer an offering to sin but an offering to God.

The second: 'This is surely cheap grace. If the law is outlawed then we can do what we like – provided we said we "believed". What a cop-out!'
Answer: This is not anarchy. Everyone serves somebody. We are slaves to sin, or we are slaves to righteousness. It's a heart matter and a true heart reveals itself in godly conduct.

A husband and wife take the stage. He, stern and unbending; she, a downtrodden and dispirited drudge – a living death. She serves Mr Law grimly and longs after the wonderful Mr Grace standing in the wings. 'If only I could die and start again,' she thinks. But it is her husband who dies. Suddenly she is free, and honourably she marries Mr Grace. Life is so different without lists of rules. Far from becoming a bad wife, inspired by the spirit of love, she takes pleasure in being the best.

The third: 'You seem to have it in for the law, but surely it is God's holy law. This sounds like blasphemy!
Answer: Of course the law isn't bad! How else would I know right from wrong? But sin hijacks the law, provoking me to sin. When the law says, 'Don't,' I find I want to. I don't understand my own actions. I know what is right and I want to do it, but I find another more powerful force driving me. What a mass of contradictions! God help me! He has; the greater power of Jesus Christ has liberated me from this spiritual schizophrenia.

Challengers answered, with the full band Paul can celebrate the glorious consequences of the gospel: 'There is now no condemnation … in Christ Jesus.' God sent Jesus, a Man who obeyed the law fully for us, so that we by the Spirit might have life.

It is the only way. Living for ourselves and our appetites always leads to death. Living by the Spirit brings life. And what a life! Our spirits are alive now, our bodies will one day follow. Already, we are children of God, heirs with Christ who instinctively cry, 'Daddy, Father!'

It's worth the price. Creation, long subjected to futility, is now in labour to birth the new age of physical and spiritual redemption. This is our hope; weak we may be, but the Spirit of God energises our prayers so that every event serves God's good purpose. Called to be like Jesus? We shall be!

We can't stop Paul now. Striding the stage in full voice he takes on all comers. God is for us, who will oppose? Christ reigns. Nothing at all in the whole universe can break the bonds of God's love in Christ Jesus our Lord.

Discussion Starters

1. Arguments arise over who, when and how people should be baptised. What do you think lies at the heart of baptism into Christ?

   _____

   _____

   _____

2. Self-image is very important in our society. In the light of Romans 6:11–14, how does our new self-image in Christ affect our behaviour?

   _____

   _____

   _____

3. We are either slaves to sin or slaves to God. How would you recommend the latter to a non-Christian hedonist?

   _____

   _____

   _____

4. The law cannot save us but it does convict us of sin. How would you apply the law to our contemporary society?

   _____

   _____

   _____

5. What difference do you think it makes to live by the law of the Spirit of life rather than the law of sin and death?

   _____

   _____

   _____

6. Paul teaches us that we can only belong to God if we have the Spirit of Christ. Why do you think this is so and how would you describe your own experience of the Spirit?

_____

_____

_____

7. Because of fear induced by bad parenting some Christians struggle with the idea of a Father God. How do you think God can heal a person from this?

_____

_____

_____

8. Creation is moving towards an omega point. What do you think this is?

_____

_____

_____

9. Many Christians find prayer difficult. In what ways does the Holy Spirit help us?

_____

_____

_____

10. Romans 8:30 has polarised some of God's people. What are the positive encouragements that we can all draw from this verse?

_____

_____

_____

Personal Application

The Christian faith is about death and resurrection rather than just a modification to our existing life. We can only experience this when we recognise that our life outside of Christ isn't worth keeping. It's time to throw away that grubby, moth-eaten, outmoded sweater, however familiar it is! Identifying ourselves with Jesus and His death ends our past, but it also inaugurates our future. Paul testifies: 'I have been crucified with Christ and I no longer live, but Christ lives in me. The life I live in the body, I live by faith in the Son of God, who loved me and gave himself for me' (Gal. 2:20). See also 2 Corinthians 5:17.

The secret of Christian living is to stay in the truth of this; it is the wonder of the exchanged life that enables us to yield our bodies to God and His service and to say 'no' to the old slave master of sin.

Seeing Jesus in the Scriptures

Jesus became sin for us on the cross; He bore the whole weight on His shoulders, He took all the guilt and condemnation, He came under its death-dealing power. In that awful time He, the purest, became the vilest. His face was distorted beyond recognition and darkness fell over the earth to hide the sight. God forsook Him, the devil gloated and hell opened its mouth.

The terrible price is fully paid. God raised His Son from the dead and exalted Him to His right hand as King of kings and Lord of lords and the source of eternal life to all who believe.

WEEK 5

Elected or Rejected?

Opening Icebreaker

Describe a moment in your life where you feel you made a wrong choice or decision that had unfortunate consequences.

Bible Readings

- Romans 9:1–11:36
- Ezekiel 36:22–38
- John 8:31–39; 15:1–8
- Galatians 6:12–13

Focus: All Israel will be saved, by grace, through faith in Christ.

Opening Our Eyes

After the crescendo, the passionate lament – a personal and heartfelt longing for the salvation of the Jewish race by one of its own choice sons.

What people these Jews are! God entrusted them with so much. Christ was born of one of their own daughters. Yet they will not believe.

Is everything lost, then? Again Abraham and Sarah take to the stage, this time with Isaac. From him run two lines: on one called 'promise' stands Jacob; on the other called 'flesh' stands Esau. Both will produce many descendants, but the salvation line runs from Jacob.

A very modern cry for equal rights comes from the wings. 'That's not fair! How can God do that?'

Actually God can do whatever He likes. He is under no obligation to accommodate our political correctness. The spotlight switches to a potter at his wheel. Some of his wares go on the meal table, others go under the bed. Can the clay dictate to the potter? No more can mortals argue with their Creator.

Anyway, there is salvation for the chamber pot. It's not by race, but by grace. Those not of the natural line may enter the spiritual line and become, equally, the children of God. It is the same for that natural line. Some of the rebellious nation have realised that racial genes cannot save and they, too, have entered into Christ by faith.

But Paul still longs for the rest of the nation. What has gone so wrong for these zealous people? They have not grasped God's way of righteousness through faith. They are attempting DIY salvation. It's futile. If only they would respond to the word of faith. Then, like the rest, they would be saved. It's not even a novel idea. Isaiah the prophet said it 700 years ago – but they are still a stubborn people.

So has God dumped them? No way, Paul answers. God doesn't give up so easily. Some, myself included, have responded. Remember that fiery prophet Elijah? Even though many Israelites to their lasting cost forsook God, a 7,000-strong remnant responded to His grace.

But surely most of the nation is beyond recovery? Paul smiles. 'I will let you into a secret,' he says. 'The unbelief of the Jews has opened the door to every other nation on earth. I hope it will make them envious! For if their rejection made salvation possible for the whole world, what would happen if they were welcomed back? Resurrection, or what!'

Anyone can write off the Jews. But learn a lesson from divine horticulture. A spreading olive tree catches our eye. Broken branches lie around it, but some wild branches have been grafted in, feeding like the remaining originals from the same rootstock. Grafted branches had best be grateful. Grow arrogant and they risk being broken off again. And imagine how well the broken originals would flourish if they were re-grafted!

So here's the heart of the divine plan: the Jews have been partially hardened to allow the other nations in, but God will yet save them. His promises do not fail. One day the nation of Israel will receive Jesus as their Messiah through faith, just like the Gentiles. The two will become one new man in Christ and so all Israel will be saved. Brilliant!

In exultant mood the full orchestra raises the roof to proclaim the sheer, unfathomable and untaught genius of God: 'From him and through him and to him are all things. To him be the glory for ever! Amen.'

31

Discussion Starters

1. Paul has a special desire to see his own people saved. What inspires us to see our own nation turn to God?

2. The Jews were very religious but their religion could not save them. What do you think are the merits of Christian salvation over and against the creeds of other religions?

3. God is good, but He isn't fair. Discuss the truth of this statement.

4. Islam implies that the will of Allah is immutable. Scientific determinism says all our choices are illusions. What are the limits of human freedom and how much does the God of the Bible give us real choices?

5. The zeal of the Jews was misplaced. How may we ensure that our own zeal is properly focused?

6. Anti-Semitism is a blight on the world. How can we believers be a ministry of reconciliation to our spiritual cousins?

_____

_____

_____

_____

7. Verbal confession and heartfelt faith are necessary for salvation. Discuss how we may bear effective witness in the world of our work and personal relationships.

_____

_____

_____

_____

8. Somebody was sent by God to share the gospel with us. What do you think makes for effective missionary work today, both at home and overseas?

_____

_____

_____

9. God is described as both stern and kind. What implications does this have for our relationship with Him?

_____

_____

_____

10. Paul's doxology in Romans 11:33–36 is inspired by God's attributes. What bearing does this have on the quality of our modern worship?

_____

_____

_____

Personal Application

Those who fight against God always lose in the end; those who humble themselves under His mighty hand find that He is full of mercy and love. It is better to fall before the Rock than to have the Rock fall on us!

It becomes us to be humble before the Lord. He is God from everlasting to everlasting. How can we ever fathom the mind of God? Surely the only appropriate response is to live our lives in worship and dependency upon Him. Humble gratitude will open the eyes of our understanding far more effectively than any amount of study and learning.

Seeing Jesus in the Scriptures

Jesus is not a pet for our convenience. We cannot make Him come from heaven at our beck and call; we cannot resurrect Him when we think He might be a useful addition to our lives. When we confess Him, we call Him Lord, that is, absolute ruler of the Universe and the Master of our own lives in particular. When we speak of His resurrection, it is because God raised Him from the dead; we did not.

Once we get this straight we can call on the name of the Lord and know that He has the power to save us. This is not misplaced trust, 'Everyone who calls on the name of the Lord will be saved.' His resurrection has granted us new life and the promise of an eternal inheritance. Faith in Christ is the best investment we can ever make. See 1 Peter 1:3–9.

WEEK 6

Love, Law and Liberty

Opening Icebreaker

Describe a situation where the behaviour of others has embarrassed or offended you.

Bible Readings

- Romans 12:1–15:13
- Matthew 7:1–5; 22:15–22
- 1 Corinthians 12:1–11
- Ephesians 4:17–32
- 1 John 3:11–24

Key verse: '… love one another, for he who loves his fellow-man has fulfilled the law.' Romans 13:8

Focus: 'Love must be sincere. Hate what is evil; cling to what is good.' Romans 12:9

Opening Our Eyes

Truth is only shown to be true when it is lived out in relation to our fellow travellers. The heights of devotion are reached when we present our bodies as a continual living sacrifice. The life of true worship has mostly to do with our attitudes to others. We take a flashback to the mass of godless humanity. Don't live like them; learn a different, transformational way of life.

A man steps onto the stage. From afar, we recognise Him as our Lord Jesus. Drawing closer we discover a composite image consisting of countless people. We cannot be followers of Christ in isolation from His Body, nor may we claim superiority over our fellow members. Each of us has received a birth gifting from God which is to be used harmoniously to bless others.

The proverbs of the good life are displayed on banners and wall plaques all around us. 'Love must be sincere.' 'Live at peace with everyone.'

A clattering mechanical monster lumbers onto the stage. The ruthless efficiency, the paranoid intolerance, the complexity and power of the State overawes us. We cannot ignore its pervasive presence. Shall we rebel and set up our own kingdom, or simply despise it?

It's on a leash! The State is only a permitted instrument of God to keep law and order. We will not worship it, but nor are we anarchists. Caesar will have his dues and we will respect his law but we live by a higher law. By loving our neighbours we fulfil the great community commandments of God.

The light shifts from the State. A coming dawn promises a greater kingdom. Leaving the paths of debauchery and division the Body of Christ clothes itself in bright armour.

It is tempting to be idealistic about the Church. Lest this happen, we draw near to a meal table. It is a tense affair. One diner is a vegetarian, another a pork-hating Jew, yet another will eat snails; beer drinkers and teetotallers sit side by side, and for some it's only fish on Fridays! Eating together is central to the life of the Church but it is a nightmare for the catering team.

It is easy to judge and to criticise; we want to impress our behaviour and our culture on others. Already voices are raised in operatic contention. Then comes Paul's persuasive pastoral calm. Let not the Church become a place of judgment on these matters. Culture is relative. Jesus died for us all. Trust one another's motives. We all serve the Lord and He alone is our judge. Be sensitive to each other's backgrounds; don't set out to offend. Remember that the kingdom of God is not a matter of food preferences 'but of righteousness, peace and joy in the Holy Spirit'. Keep a sense of perspective and do everything in faith.

Most especially look after one another. Those who feel strong must build up the weak. We don't just please ourselves. Paul sinks into an attitude of prayer. God grant us such a unity in our diversity that we may worship with one heart and voice. Christ has accepted us; accept one another. Remember that your Jewish brethren are here because of God's promises to the patriarchs, and your Gentile brethren because of His promises to bless the whole world. Let's then sing the benediction together: 'May the God of hope fill you with all joy and peace as you trust in him, so that you may overflow with hope by the power of the Holy Spirit.'

Discussion Starters

1. Acts of worship are often limited to liturgical rituals and congregational singing. What do we need to do to make our entire lives an act of worship?

   _____
   _____
   _____

2. God has granted each of us a measure of faith. How can we best put those measures together for the greater good?

   _____
   _____
   _____

3. Jesus told us to love our enemies. How might we be instruments of God's peace in this combative and troubled world?

   _____
   _____
   _____

4. 'We must obey God rather than man.' What are the limits to the obedience that we should render to the State?

   _____
   _____
   _____

5. All you need is love has become the mantra for judging behaviour on the basis of how it feels. What is the relationship between love and ethical absolutes?

   _____
   _____
   _____

6. The kingdom of God is coming and we are to rise to

the day. What does it mean to put on the armour of light?

_____

_____

_____

7. Most divisions between Christians are over culture rather than doctrine. What steps can we take to enhance our unity with believers from different traditions to our own?

_____

_____

_____

8. Some matters of conduct are subjective and second- ary; others are of primary importance. How do we distinguish between matters of individual conscience and matters of non-negotiable principle?

_____

_____

_____

9. This is an age of food fads and dietary concerns when we worry about poisoning ourselves and believe that food affects our behaviour. How can we eat wisely but maintain our kingdom focus on righteousness, peace and joy in the Holy Spirit?

_____

_____

_____

10. Christian love means not tyrannising one another by our behaviour nor imposing that behaviour on others. What do you think are the practical keys to exercising this kind of tolerance?

_____

_____

_____

Personal Application

What we believe determines our behaviour. The great doctrine of justification by faith provides us with a grace foundation for our conduct. We must live this out in three interrelated spheres: that of the Body of Christ, that of the State and that of everyday humanity. Within the Body we are to exercise unity, love and tolerance within the bounds of the great ethical commandments. We are to treat the State with respect as law-abiding citizens, but Caesar cannot be our Lord and Master. We are to be a source of blessing to our non-believing relatives, friends, neighbours and colleagues, while at the same time refraining from their sins.

All this is made possible by us continually presenting our bodies to the service of God as those who are profoundly grateful for His mercy.

Seeing Jesus in the Scriptures

A reading of the Gospels demonstrates that in all respects Jesus lived His life by grace and truth. He is the perfect example of all that Paul writes in these verses. Nowhere is this clearer than in His generous acceptance of people that others found offensive. Think of the social outcasts and people of loose morals that sought His help.

Paul tells us that this is because Jesus saw Himself as a servant to the people and not their master. Jesus said, 'For even the Son of Man did not come to be served, but to serve, and to give his life as a ransom for many' (Mark 10:45). We should pray that we may have the same attitude in the spheres of our personal relationships.

WEEK 7

Traveller's Tales

Opening Icebreaker

Describe something that you really admire and appreciate in the person sitting next to you.

Bible Readings

- Romans 15:14–16:27
- Matthew 28:16–20
- John 17:13–26
- 1 Corinthians 12:12–31

Key verse: 'I myself am convinced, my brothers, that you yourselves are full of goodness …' Romans 15:14

Focus: 'I commend … greet one another …' Romans 16:1, 16

Opening Our Eyes

It's time for the credits to roll. Paul is the gospel messenger, the writer/performer of this opera, and he takes centre stage to say a few personal words. He makes no falsely apologetic noises – as if a virtuoso performer would pretend he could only fiddle about with a few notes! He has a calling, a priestly task to bring the Gentiles into a place of acceptance with God. Yet his glory is wholly in Christ and he will not boast of his own achievements. It has been the power of the Holy Spirit at work that has wrought all the miracles and signs. This modest man has profound convictions and a stupendous track record, but he shows no trace of ego.

The video unfolds and we scan vast stretches of land: cities, villages, mountains and valleys, seaports and synagogues; Paul has preached the gospel from Jerusalem to the Adriatic, and always on virgin territory lest he find himself competing with other apostles. It has been a mammoth task but it is now essentially completed. Churches are in place. The message will flourish through their witness.

Now that rugged outpost of the Western world, the Spanish peninsular, beckons and Paul plans to visit Rome on the way. However, he explains, he has one task to complete. In the midst of his gospel preaching throughout the Gentile world he has been raising money to relieve the poverty of the believers based in Jerusalem. It will be a dangerous trip. Paul has enemies among his own people, Jewish fundamentalists who will be after his life. He requests prayer for protection.

Sometimes it is tempting to see Paul as a strong individualist, a somewhat scary character happy in his own company. Nothing could be further from the truth.

He is a warm, passionate team player. There is scarcely a moment in his ministry when he is not working with a large team of men and women who share the same love for Jesus. So he ends with a list of these dear friends who have laboured alongside him and who have travelled far and wide for the sake of the gospel. Many have evidently found their way to Rome and he sends his fond greetings to them along with his personal commendations.

First, Phoebe, the woman entrusted with delivering and reading this letter, then people like Priscilla and Aquila who have risked their lives, then members of Paul's own family and fellow apostles, hardworking servants of Jesus. Paul reminds the Roman believers to greet one another with affection and he sends them greetings from all the churches of Christ.

These people are an example of unity in the gospel. There are others around, those who have leapt on to the personality bandwagon, who lift money from the gullible, who speak against true servants of God in order to boost their own reputation. Don't attend their meetings or support their ministries! Don't allow anyone to spoil your purity in Christ. The God of peace will soon crush Satan under your feet. You don't need any flashy egotists to help you.

A few more greetings follow, including those of Paul's secretary, Tertius, and his generous hosts in Corinth. All that remains is the apostolic blessing, and a reminder that this gospel of Jesus Christ is a mighty prophetic fulfilment. He signs off with a final acclamation of the glory of God through Jesus Christ and a resounding Amen whose echo will be felt right down to our present day.

Discussion Starters

1. The apostle Paul is often portrayed as a misogynist academic; quite contrary to how the Bible reveals him. How might we present Paul in a fairer light so that people could receive the revelation that God gave through him?

   _____

   _____

2. Paul most likely did take the gospel to Spain. What people groups in your own country and abroad still need to hear the gospel? What part might you play in this?

   _____

   _____

3. Paul preached the gospel and collected money for the poor. What does this teach us about sharing the gospel in our own society?

   _____

   _____

4. Paul prays and often asks for prayer. How can we be effective prayer partners with those who proclaim the gospel?

   _____

   _____

5. Paul clearly honours the ministry of both men and women. In one or two other places he indicates that some ministries are inappropriate for women. Why was this, and does it have a bearing on ministry today?

   _____

   _____

6. Paul and his team took great risks to preach the gospel. When is it right to act in the face of the law and at what point would you find it necessary to do so?

_____

_____

7. The ministry of hospitality is among the highest in Paul's estimation. In an age when our homes are private fortresses how can we exercise this ministry in a biblical manner?

_____

_____

8. The Early Church had its fair share of self-seeking false apostles. With global access to a wide variety of ministries what tests of discernment should we apply?

_____

_____

9. Christians are called to engage in spiritual warfare. What does Paul mean when he talks of God crushing Satan beneath our feet?

_____

_____

10. Many of Paul's benedictions have been formalised in our church services. Try writing a benediction for your group meeting.

_____

_____

Personal Application

Fellowship with one another is a key concept throughout this letter and the quality of relationships was clearly paramount to the success of the work. We often invent projects and then try to find 'volunteers', to fill the slots, whereas a biblical world-view would suggest that first we find the people and let them determine what God would have them do together.

Effective service arises from a combination of good leadership and team work where love for one another conditions and sweetens our working relationship. We should all be able to name our key 'fellowship in service' relationships. Are these as harmonious as they should be or should we give some attention to building those friendships onto a better foundation?

Seeing Jesus in the Scriptures

Jesus formed His own team of apostles and friends. In numerous places Paul talks about us being 'in the Lord' or 'in Christ'. This is more than a metaphor; we are literally one new man in Christ. He is the Head; we are the Body. Together we are the hands and feet of the Lord. Not one of us is the whole ministry of Christ. To behave as a loner is to distance ourselves from both the Head and the Body, in effect making ourselves the head of our own body – a false Christ and a false church with a membership of one!

When we live and serve in Christ, He works in and through us all for His good pleasure and the glory goes quite properly to Him rather than to anyone else.

Leader's Notes

Week 1: Good News or What?

Open this first session by reading the Introduction. The idea is to capture the imagination of your group members so that they can anticipate beginning a spiritual adventure that will prove startlingly relevant to their contemporary world.

Members of the group need to understand the text, but they most especially need to experience the power of this truth in their daily lives.

You will not always get through all the Discussion Starters, especially if you have a talkative group. Try to involve as many as possible and to keep the discussion earthed in reality. A devotional atmosphere should pervade the gathering.

Because the main readings are of necessity quite long passages it will help if two or three people read a section each, though preferably from the same version. Alternatively, you may wish the group to read the main passage in advance of the meeting and then to read the supplementary scriptures when you meet.

Opening Icebreaker

All the icebreakers are designed to relate to the main passage of Scripture under consideration. This first one is about good news and it will provide an easy way for everyone to share something of their own life experience. Apart from the obvious things, good news can also be something *not* happening such as a favourable medical report or the job you *didn't* get.

Aim of the Session

We want to capture something of the excitement and sense of dynamism that Paul felt in his heart. This message is good news for everyone on earth and its all about Jesus. Remind the group of this by using Discussion Starters 2 & 3. You may wish to read the Seeing Jesus in the Scriptures section at this point. I often describe myself to not-yet-believers as a dedicated fan of Jesus rather than as a Christian. It helps overcome the negative connotations often associated with that word.

The Christian faith is a movement and when it ceases to be so it becomes a mausoleum. Using Discussion Starter 1, try to draw out the apostolic mandate that lies at the heart of our faith. The word *apostolos* means messenger. Its Latin translation gives us the word *missionary* but that is often debased from its primary meaning of someone who does what Paul and his companions did.

The apostolic foundation implies that we are all called upon to share our faith with others. Use Discussion Starters 7, 8 & 10 to open up how we should respond to this in our own day. Discussion Starter 9 will help us talk about just how much or how little our friends and colleagues are capable of understanding.

Paul writes his letter as a man of great enthusiasm and personal commitment. True servants of Christ do not simply have a message to deliver; they are possessed by their message. Use Discussion Starters 4–6 to explore how much we are sold out on the gospel in our own lives.

Personal Application

Some, for a variety of reasons, may be feeling discouraged. If the session has gone as it should then the group will be stirred to a new enthusiasm for the gospel.

Offer an opportunity for prayer to those who are wavering.

Many of us feel inadequate when it comes to personal witness, yet this is how the majority of people become followers of Christ. Take time to pray for boldness, wisdom and opportunity to make Jesus known.

Week 2: As Guilty as Hell

Opening Icebreaker

This icebreaker is meant to be fun, which is why we are interested in childhood pranks rather than adult crimes! It will be interesting to ask people why they felt guilty. Whom did they feel they were letting down? Whose laws were they transgressing?

Aim of the Session

This passage provides us with one of the most honest analyses of human nature in the Bible, yet it flies right in the face of the Western liberal establishment. By using Discussion Starter 9 you will discover just how much the group has been influenced by secular sociology and psychology. It may surprise you all!

In this section Paul traces a tragic downward path from the glories of our Creator God into the depths of a wilful idolatry that leaves us God-forsaken. Human depravity takes centre stage. Using Discussion Starters 1 & 3 encourage the group to talk about the inevitable consequences of denying God as Creator. The con-sequences of Social Darwinism were catastrophic in the twentieth century, fuelling political totalitarianism and multinational imperialism alike.

Human beings cannot help worshipping. When we

forsake God we worship idols instead. Those idols may be our enthusiasms such as a football team or a rock group; they may be our homes, cars and other material obsessions; they may be people whom we adulate, or private obsessive habits such as watching Internet porn. Use Discussion Starter 2 to identify where our idols lie.

Religion is our attempt to please God, yet even the best religion cannot solve the problems of human behaviour. It leads inevitably to hypocrisy. Use Discussion Starter 4 and look at the context in Matthew 7 to check out our own hypocrisy index.

Judaism is the finest religion in the world. Its law, the Ten Commandments in particular, set the highest moral tone, and yet the law cannot save us. Using Discussion Starters 5–8 & 10 explore the reasons why salvation cannot be attained by self-help.

Discussing the depravity of the human heart will be likely to remind some members of the group of their own misdemeanours. Some will feel guilty for good reasons; some unnecessarily so. It is important that we deal with each appropriately and that we don't just pour out plat-itudes. The gospel exposes real sin but provides a real remedy. Take a look at 1 John 1:5–10 for some additional help. If you have a not-yet-believer in your group this may be an opportunity to invite a response to faith.

All of us need reminding that real holiness is attractive and if we wear our religion in a way that makes people think we are smug, judgmental, faultfinding hypocrites, then we certainly don't have the religion of Jesus!

Week 3: Faith's Big Daddy

Opening Icebreaker

Most of us can point out the shortcomings of our earthly fathers and for some those problems are extremely serious. Be prepared for one or more members of your group to say that they admired nothing because their father was non-existent in their lives. A badly abused person may wish not to participate in this icebreaker. Others will have very positive things to say and we should concentrate on these with the intent of seeing that fatherhood is God's good idea.

Aim of the Session

This session brings us face to face with the enormity of the cross of Christ. Our sins put Him there. He died as the just for the unjust to bring us to God. This is the classic doctrine of substitutionary atonement. Paul puts it succinctly in 2 Corinthians 5:21: 'God made him who had no sin to be sin for us, so that in him we might become the righteousness of God.' Use Discussion Starters 1–4 to ensure that everyone really understands this. Some Christians seem almost to embrace the ancient Marcionite heresy of proposing that the Old Testament God or Demiurge is different from the New Testament God. This may be a good opportunity to discuss just what we mean by God. God didn't become God and God didn't become love on the opening page of the New Testament. He is God from everlasting and His character does not change with the turning of the pages!

Abraham is our spiritual father, the fountainhead of a new breed of human who, depending on their family tree, may or may not be able to trace their earthly bloodline back to him but who can most certainly trace their spiritual bloodline to him because they share his faith. Use

Discussion Starter 5 to explore what this means.

Abraham is a marvellous example of faith and perseverance. In an age of instant results, and especially for
the ageing existentialists in our midst, we need to learn
these lessons. Use Discussion Starters 6–8 to draw out the
importance of both faithfulness and 'full-of-faith-ness'.

If Abraham is the father of the line of faith, we must
remember that his faith was in Christ. Jesus said of
Abraham that he 'rejoiced at the thought of seeing my
day; he saw it and was glad' (John 8:56). Adam brought
ruin upon the world because of his disobedience. Jesus
brings blessing because of His obedience to God's will.
Use Discussion Starters 9 & 10 to talk about the qual-
ifications of Jesus as our new federal Head. Comparing
Him to a tribal founder may be helpful.

Assurance of salvation is elusive for some people, most
often because of bad teaching in the past or lack of
experiencing the Holy Spirit in a meaningful way in their
lives. Read the Personal Application section to help such
people focus on the sufficiency of Christ rather than their
own sense of unworthiness. Remind them that we are all
unworthy – that is why Christ died. Try to help people
understand that faith in Christ is not complicated.
Provided that we have put our faith in Him, knowing the
exact date is not important, nor are the feelings we may
have had. If you really want to believe in Christ then it is
a sign that you do believe and are therefore saved!

Finally, focus on the Seeing Jesus in the Scriptures section
and refer to the reading from Hebrews chap 5. Stress the
betterness of the new covenant over the old and take the
opportunity to offer praise and thanksgiving to Jesus for
all that He has done to open up the way of salvation for
the peoples of all nations.

Week 4: Wanted Dead and Alive

Opening Icebreaker

This may be an excuse for tall stories, quite a few of which may involve driving cars! Some will have serious tales to tell. Encourage each one present to speak about how they feel about dying.

Aim of the Session

It is not possible to be a follower of Jesus without dying to our self-interest, or ego. Unless that happens we shall remain slaves to sin. Once it has then we are free to serve righteousness. We are never free to do as we please – nobody is. Using Discussion Starters 1–4, try to ensure that the members of the group have really understood this. It is the key to Christian behaviour. Read the Personal Application and Seeing Jesus in the Scriptures sections to help people understand their new identity in Christ. Over-coming behaviour problems, old habits and temptations is done not by a head-to-head confrontation but by showing our new identity card. We are in Christ; threaten us and you have to take on Jesus as well!

Grace appears to find itself at loggerheads with the law, yet Paul is not negating the law, rather he is bringing in a higher law – in much the same way as the laws of aerodynamics transcend the law of gravity. This higher law is that of the Spirit of life. Use the passage in Galatians 5 to help people grasp the principle that if we walk by the Spirit then we cannot and will not at the same time fulfil the cravings of a selfish nature. People vary in their experiences of the Holy Spirit much as they do with everything else. What matters is that we know the power and witness of the Spirit in our lives, never mind too much how we got there. Use Discussion Starters 5 & 6 to help this discussion.

We return with Discussion Starter 7 to this issue of father-hood. The highest privilege granted to us is that we may have a personal relationship with God the Father. It may be that some in the group, because of bad ex-periences, would appreciate prayer in this area. The answer lies not in avoiding the fatherhood of God, but in realising that He at least gets it right and that He can restore the missing dimension to our lives.

From our personal intimate experience of God, Paul takes us to a cosmic perspective. All of creation awaits the unveiling of the sons of God, that is, we shall all be seen for what we are in Christ at the end of time when He returns. Try not to become too entangled with end-time theories and speculative charts of future events. Con-centrate instead on the glory to come. Remind folk also that although the death of Christ accomplished everything necessary for our salvation, as the Risen One He both celebrates the glory of God's creation and, at the same time, He is longing and working for its ultimate redemp-tion, He enters empathetically into its pain. Our own trials and our prayers of longing are part of those continuing sufferings of Christ that will bring to birth a new age when all evil is abolished. Use Discussion Starters 8 & 9 to help focus this point.

Discussion Starter 10 invites us to have a fight over our differing understandings of election and predestination. Or, we may settle for glorying in the awesome plan and purposes of God that, in spite of all our failings, will one day succeed in bringing about the reconciliation of all things in Christ!

Week 5: Elected or Rejected?

Opening Icebreaker
It is sometimes hard to admit that we make mistakes but
we all do. The group may now be able to share honestly
about their misjudgments. These might include failed
relationships, wrong career moves or a poor purchase.
Choices about faith have far more profound consequences
for our lives.

Aim of the Session
The subject matter concerns the relationship between the
Jews and the gospel and the salvation of the Gentiles. It
raises all the big questions about God's election and the
place of human response; it also makes us look at the
often questionable and at times scandalous attitude of the
Church towards the Jews.

The scenario is simple enough: the Jews were chosen
by God as the vehicle of salvation. Most but not all of
them refused their Messiah Jesus and the grace offer
of salvation through faith in Him. Their rejection, already
anticipated by God, has opened the door for the Gentiles
to be saved. Nevertheless, because God keeps His
promises, one day the Jews as a whole will be saved.
It will be on the same faith–grace basis as the Gentiles,
just like Paul and other Jews in the believing remnant.
Meanwhile the Gentiles need to recognise that they
are privileged to be allowed in on what was once a
Jewish preserve, and on such advantageous terms!
Use Discussion Starter 6 to open up the question about
our attitude towards the Jews.

Christianity, except in its most superficial aspects, is not
a religion but a partnership between us and God – albeit
not an equal partnership! The fact that God is knowable

and that we can speak about a personal intimacy with Him that is more than merely emotional stillness or transcendent awe is what distinguishes our faith from other religions. Use Discussion Starters 1 & 2 to talk about the place of that kind of faith in a multicultural society. You may then wish to use Discussion Starters 5, 7 & 8 to explore and encourage the vital role of our personal witness in the world of our everyday relationships in the home, the workplace and the community.

The problem of human freedom and divine sovereignty raises questions about our perceptions of what God is really like. We live in an age when, in democracies, the rights of the individual are paramount and the task of government is to safeguard those rights while at the same time seeking to ensure that we respect the parameters of others' rights. It does not have the right to dictate to our wills. How much does this mentality colour our attitude towards God? When the early believers met for a significant prayer meeting (Acts 4:24–31), they addressed God by the title 'Despot' ('Sovereign Lord' in the NIV). Use Discussion Starters 3, 4 & 9 to explore the right of God to do as He wills and the degree to which He grants us genuine freedom of choice. It will be helpful at this point to read the Personal Application and Seeing Jesus in the Scriptures sections.

The doxology, properly celebrating as it does God's infinite splendour, concludes Paul's major thesis. All true theology provokes worship in the hearts of believers, worship of God for His own sake. Sadly much of contemporary worship is subjective and the degree to which we honour God seems to depend on the qualities of the worship leader and whether or not we have had a good week. How we feel – the truth about us – pales into insignificance when we concentrate on the truth about Him. Use Discussion Starter 10 to remind us of this.

Week 6: Love, Law and Liberty

Opening Icebreaker

This one should be fun! Telling these tales often helps
us to see that our own sense of offence was unnecessary
and over the top. God uses these events much as the
Court Jester, to stop the king from taking himself too
seriously.

Aim of the Session

This session begins with one of the great 'therefores'
of the Bible. If all this is true then it has profound and
practical implications for how we must behave. Jews and
Gentiles are justified by faith alone. They constitute one
new man in Christ. He alone is Lord, not the State, not
anybody. Since there is no superior race, we must love
our neighbour and especially tolerate our cultural
differences. A Jew does not have to take on a Gentile
culture nor a Gentile a Jewish culture. Culture does not
save us; Christ does. So be in unity around Him and
everything else will work out. Eating together is fund-
amental to fellowship and should be at the heart of
church life, something that has been rediscovered in
evangelistic contexts such as Alpha courses but needs to
extend into every part of our shared life in Christ. It is
here that we work out those cultural differences. With
whom shall we eat? Only those like ourselves or with
anyone in the family of God? Use Discussion Starters 7–10
to explore this and other matters of culture. Be careful to
avoid protracted discussions about food preferences and
the environment lest we fall into the very trap we are
trying to avoid!

Believers are granted gifts from God, not for their personal merit or advancement, but for the service of others.
Using Discussion Starter 2 and being as practical as

possible, encourage the members of the group to be forthcoming about their gifts and the measure of faith that they think they have in the exercise of those gifts. It may well be that two or more might work together to achieve a greater good.

The Church must live out its faith in an often hostile environment. The State usurps its powers in many parts of the world and even in the West we live at a time when the State is more intrusive than ever before. Use Discussion Starters 3–6 to open up this subject. Be careful to avoid party politics but don't be afraid to talk about politics. The term kingdom of God, *basileia tou theou,* i.e. God's government, is thoroughly political. Ensure that you spend most of this time discussing the common behavioural issues that arise as we seek to express our faith in a relativist and perverse culture.

Read the Personal Application section and use Discussion Starter 1 to focus on our daily devotion to God. This is measured not only by our times of prayer and Bible reading, or by the number of spiritual songs that we sing, but by the constant offering of our physical bodies in sacrificial service to the Lord. This is our practical response to our new status in Christ. Free from our status in Adam we may now willingly choose to serve the Lord. In so doing, we discover the brilliance of God's will for our lives. Draw out what this might mean during an average working day. Conclude by reading the Seeing Jesus in the Scriptures section and encourage one another to have the same servant-hearted spirit of love as He did.

Week 7: Traveller's Tales

Opening Icebreaker

This is an invitation for us to express appreciation of one another, something we do too little of in our culture. Encourage people to think positively about this and allow no 'buts' that might diminish the compliments.

Aim of the Session

This session allows us an insight into the fellowship of Paul's team of workers. We discover, spanning many years, a world of warm and sacrificial relationships coupled with a passion for the gospel. This is quite a different picture from the one often presented by our secular educators who, feeling threatened by the intellectual and personal challenge of Paul's writings, want to parody his character as a politically correct way of dismissing him. Use Discussion Starters 1 & 5 to tackle people's misconceptions. Some want to say that Paul's writings are just his ideas; yet the Holy Spirit inspired Paul just as much as Isaiah or Matthew. All that we have read came to the apostle by divine revelation during his three-year retreat into Arabia – see Galatians 1:11–18.

The Early Church was a missionary movement and the Church was shaped accordingly. This is something we must recapture in terms both of our own nation and of the global community. Use Discussion Starters 2–4 to explore how we may effectively reach every man, woman and child on the planet with an incarnational, repeated and thorough presentation of the gospel.

Teamwork was clearly vital to the spread of the gospel. Paul had a considerable number of companions, some of whom were with him long-term and others for shorter periods. Much of our evangelism fails because either it is done by individuals or because the church leadership has come up with a project for which it then seeks volunteers. A better approach is to bring together those who can form resonant relationships and then allow them to find out what God has in mind for them to do.

Where there is truth there is falsehood. In Paul's time there were self-seeking itinerant apostles who tried to con God's people. There were those who wanted to adulterate the gospel of grace with the addition of circumcision and Jewish ritualism. If they had succeeded then the Christian faith would have faded out as just another short-lived sect of Judaism. Use Discussion Starter 8 to coax out from the group what they believe to be the right principles of spiritual discernment.

There was also a growing opposition from the State that was eventually to break out in full-scale systematic per-secution around AD 64. Use Discussion Starters 6 & 9 to remind us of the need to fight the good fight of the faith. It might be good to remember in prayer those who suffer for their faith in various parts of the world.

We are in this world to be a blessing to others. That includes using our resources to help the needy. Discussion Starter 7 will raise the matter of how we view our poss-essions and the extent to which we are prepared to open up our lives to others. You could read the Personal Application and Seeing Jesus sections after this.

We end this series of studies with Discussion Starter 10. Good news leads to good words. You may wish to ask each member of the group to write their own benediction for the group and then get each of them to read in turn so as to make a group blessing – a most appropriate way of ending the series!

National Distributors

UK: (and countries not listed below)
CWR, Waverley Abbey House, Waverley Lane, Farnham, Surrey GU9 8EP.
Tel: (01252) 784710 Outside UK (44) 1252 784710

AUSTRALIA: CMC Australasia, PO Box 519, Belmont, Victoria 3216.
Tel: (03) 5241 3288

CANADA: Cook Communications Ministries, PO Box 98, 55 Woodslee Avenue, Paris, Ontario Tel: 1800 263 2664

GHANA: Challenge Enterprises of Ghana, PO Box 5723, Accra.
Tel: (021) 222437/223249 Fax: (021) 226227

HONG KONG: Cross Communications Ltd, 1/F, 562A Nathan Road, Kowloon.
Tel: 2780 1188 Fax: 2770 6229

INDIA: Crystal Communications, 10-3-18/4/1, East Marredpally, Secunderabad – 500 026.
Tel/Fax: (040) 7732801

KENYA: Keswick Books and Gifts Ltd, PO Box 10242, Nairobi.
Tel: (02) 331692/226047 Fax: (02) 728557

MALAYSIA: Salvation Book Centre (M) Sdn Bhd, 23 Jalan SS 2/64,
47300 Petaling Jaya, Selangor.
Tel: (03) 78766411/78766797 Fax: (03) 78757066/78756360

NEW ZEALAND: CMC Australasia, PO Box 36015, Lower Hutt.
Tel: 0800 449 408 Fax: 0800 449 049

NIGERIA: FBFM, Helen Baugh House, 96 St Finbarr's College Road, Akoka, Lagos.
Tel: (01) 7747429/4700218/825775/827264

PHILIPPINES: OMF Literature Inc, 776 Boni Avenue, Mandaluyong City.
Tel: (02) 531 2183 Fax: (02) 531 1960

REPUBLIC OF IRELAND: Scripture Union, 40 Talbot Street, Dublin 1.
Tel: (01) 8363764

SINGAPORE: Armour Publishing Pte Ltd, Block 203A Henderson Road,
11–06 Henderson Industrial Park, Singapore 159546.
Tel: 6 276 9976 Fax: 6 276 7564

SOUTH AFRICA: Struik Christian Books, 80 MacKenzie Street,
PO Box 1144, Cape Town 8000.
Tel: (021) 462 4360 Fax: (021) 461 3612

SRI LANKA: Christombu Books, 27 Hospital Street, Colombo 1.
Tel: (01) 433142/328909

TANZANIA: CLC Christian Book Centre, PO Box 1384, Mkwepu Street, Dar es Salaam.
Tel/Fax: (022) 2119439

USA: Cook Communications Ministries, PO Box 98, 55 Woodslee Avenue,
Paris, Ontario, Canada.
Tel: 1800 263 2664

ZIMBABWE: Word of Life Books, Shop 4, Memorial Building,
35 S Machel Avenue, Harare.
Tel: (04) 781305 Fax: (04) 774739

For email addresses, visit the CWR website: www.cwr.org.uk
CWR is a registered charity – number 294387

Trusted
All Over the World

Daily Devotionals

Books and Videos

Day and Residential Courses

Counselling Training

Biblical Study Courses

Regional Seminars

Ministry to Women

CWR have been providing training and resources for Christians since the 1960s. From our headquarters at Waverley Abbey House we have been serving God's people with a vision to help apply God's Word to everyday life and relationships. The daily devotional *Every Day with Jesus* is read by over three-quarters of a million people in more than 150 countries, and our unique courses in biblical studies and pastoral care are respected all over the world.

For a free brochure about our seminars and courses or a catalogue of CWR resources please contact us at the following address:

CWR,
Waverley Abbey House,
Waverley Lane,
Farnham,
Surrey GU9 8EP

Telephone: 01252 784700
Email: mail@cwr.org.uk
Website: www.cwr.org.uk

CWR   CRUSADE FOR WORLD REVIVAL   *Applying God's Word to everyday life and relatior*

Cover to Cover
Bible Study Guides

These Bible guides from the *Cover to Cover* series, have been created to provide a unique resource for group and individual study lasting between one and two hours. Seven stimulating sessions in each book, supported by opening icebreakers, Bible references, discussion starters and suggestions for personal application.

The Image of God
His Attributes and Character
ISBN: 1-85345-228-9

The Tabernacle
Entering into God's Presence
ISBN: 1-85345-230-0

The Uniqueness of our Faith
What makes Christianity Distinctive?
ISBN: 1-85345-232-7

Ruth
Loving Kindness in Action
ISBN: 1-85345-231-9

Mark
Life as it is Meant to be Lived
ISBN: 1-85345-233-5

Ephesians
Claiming your Inheritance
ISBN: 1-85345-229-7

£3.49 each

The Kingdom
Studies from Matthew's Gospel
ISBN: 1-85345-251-3

The Letter to the Romans
Good news for everyone
ISBN: 1-85345-250-5

The Covenants
God's promises and
their relevance today
ISBN: 1-85345-255-6

Joseph
The power of forgiveness
and reconciliation
ISBN: 1-85345-252-1

Great Prayers of the Bible
Applying them to our lives today
ISBN: 1-85345-253-X

The Holy Spirit
Understanding and experiencing Him
ISBN: 1-85345-254-8

£3.49 each